WALKING TOWARD MORNING

WALKING TOWARD MORNING

Meditations

Victoria Safford

SKINNER HOUSE BOOKS
BOSTON

Copyright © 2003 by Victoria Safford. All rights reserved. Published by Skinner House Books. Skinner House Books is an imprint of the Unitarian Universalist Association, a liberal religious organization with more than 1,000 congregations in the U.S. and Canada. 25 Beacon Street, Boston, MA 02108-2800.

Printed in Canada.

Cover design by Kimberly Glyder.

Text design by Suzanne Morgan.

ISBN 1-55896-454-1

Library of Congress Cataloging-in-Publication Data

Safford, Victoria.
    Walking toward morning / Victoria Safford.
       p. cm.
   ISBN 1-55896-454-1 (alk. paper)
  1. Creation—Meditations. 2. Nature—Religious aspects. 3. Spiritual life. I. Title.
BL227.S24 2003
242—dc21   2003042708

For Keith and Joanna Van Antwerp

and

the members of
White Bear Unitarian Universalist Church
with respect and gratitude

Contents

Walking Toward Morning   1

Call to Worship   2

Solid Ground   3

God Is What Knows How to Grow   5

The Wind Is Bearing Me Across the Sky   7

Efficiency   9

At One   11

Turquoise Patriot   13

Any Other Questions?   15

Who Do You Think You Are?   17

Stung by Bees   19

The Gold Stars and the Bittersweet   21

Table Blessing   23

Subversive Suburban Soul   25

Trees for Starters   27

Open Eyes   29

In Between   31

Immortal, Invisible   33

Set in Stone   35

The Moment of Magic   37

In the Struggle, Singing, Shining   39

Why Do You Come, John?   41

Women Walking in Loud Shoes   43

Memory   45

Incarnation   47

If I Were Asked   49

Desert Spring   51

Did the Sun Come Up This Morning?   53

Necessities   55

Map of the Journey in Progress   57

Credo for Now   59

Unitarian Universalist Meditation Manuals   61

Walking Toward Morning

You know, we do it every day. Every morning we go out blinking into the glare of our freedom, into the wilderness of work and the world, making maps as we go, looking for signs that we're on the right path. And on some good days we walk right out of our oppressions, those things that press us down from the outside or (as often) from the inside; we shake off the shackles of fear, prejudice, timidity, closed-mindedness, selfishness, self-righteousness, and claim our freedom outright, terrifying as it is—our freedom to be human, and humane.

Every morning, every day, we leave our houses, not knowing if it will be for the last time, and we decide what we'll take with us, what we'll carry: how much integrity, how much truth-telling, how much compassion (in case somebody along the way may need some), how much arrogance, how much anger, how much humor, how much willingness to change and to be changed, to grow and to be grown. How much faith and hope, how much love and gratitude—you pack these with your lunch and medications, your date book and your papers. Every day, we gather what we think we'll need, pick up what we love and all that we so far believe, put on our history, shoulder our experience and memory, take inventory of our blessings, and we start walking toward morning.

Call to Worship

What if there were a universe, a cosmos, which began in shining blackness, out of nothing, out of fire, out of a single, silent breath, and into it came billions and billions of stars, stars beyond imagining, and near one of them a world, a blue-green world so beautiful that learned clergymen could not even speak about it cogently, and brilliant scientists, with their physics, their mathematics, their empirical, impressionistic musing, in trying to describe it, would begin to sound like poets?

What if there were a universe in which a world was born out of a smallish star, and into that world (at some point) flew red-winged blackbirds, and into it swam sperm whales, and into it bloomed crocuses, and into it blew wind to lift the tiniest hairs on naked arms in spring, and into it at some point grew onions, out of soil, and in went Mt. Everest and also the coyote we've spotted in the woods about a mile from here, just after sunrise on these mornings when the moon is full? (The very scent of him makes his brother, our dog, insane with fear and joy and ancient inbred memory.) Into that world came animals and elements and plants, and imagination, the mind and the mind's eye. If such a universe existed and you noticed it, what would you do? What song would come out of your mouth, what prayer, what praises, what sacred offering, what whirling dance, what religion and what reverential gesture would you make to greet that world, every single day that you were in it?

Solid Ground

We were packing to move, and invited several moving companies to come to the house and look at our stuff and give estimates on hauling it all halfway across the continent. Big, hulking men came tramping through, assessing the meaning of our furniture and books and little treasures in a way that we ourselves had never tried: by weight. With the flick of a cigar, one guy said dismissively, "I figure you're not worth more than 14,000 pounds." No one had ever told me that before.

The movers all noticed something a little weird about our home. On the windowsills, on the kitchen table, on my desk upstairs, by the bedsides, on the counters, even on the edge of the bathtub, we had quite a lot of rocks. Dozens and dozens of smooth, cool stones weighty with age, worn round by salt water, and all the little pebbles, kicked for miles and pocketed on hikes, were moving now (and also, by the way and for the record: chestnuts, pine cones, shells, feathers, a dead horseshoe crab as large as a skillet, bits of driftwood and various sticks, mica sheets, animal bones and an interesting fossil, leaves pressed in wax paper, and a small branch complete with acorns, found gently draped across the grave, in Concord, of Henry David Thoreau). All of it was moving. I don't know the cost per pound of carting all these things out of their element across eight states, but I do know their worth. These pieces from the ground, pieces borrowed from familiar and beloved ground, these pieces of the earth, ground me.

And here's a strange thing. Toward the end of our packing I became less careful, and instead of setting big heavy rocks with big heavy rocks, and delicate shells with other shells, and feathers with feathers, and so on, in some boxes I just tossed a lot of stuff together. Unpacking at the other end, I found in the bottom of those boxes, with mouse skulls and starfish and sticks still intact, DIRT. Dirt made not of rock alone but of things once alive, some only lately alive, fish and birds and mammals breathing, plants green and moist and succulent, bones and shells with blood or sticky substances attached. In the bottom of the boxes, it all became soil, as most things will if you are patient.

There is a kind of comfort in the certainty that even we are nothing, dust to dust, and that we are essentially, eternally, all things.

Homesick and hopeful in a new house filled with boxes, in the middle of the Midwest, in the middle of midlife, I wondered on the floor one August afternoon, *Where have we come from and where are we going? What binds us to each other? Where is our common, solid ground?*

God Is What Knows How to Grow

The story is older than the *Story of Salvation*. It begins in that event, that moment, that split second of light (or music or love, or fire, whatever it was) when matter and energy and being explode out of the pinpoint of no-being. For me the story begins behind the velvet curtain that separates what we know from Mystery. This is the story of the universe, the cosmology of stars and suns and life and no-life, all of which I call creation, even though I know of no creator. (Recently, I read that in the Hopi language there are no nouns like these, only verb forms, to describe such things, so all of this, all the cosmos, would be called "creating," and I think I like that better.) It is not a human-centered story; human history is part of something larger, more eternal and more infinite.

But ours is the laughing part of the story, the sorrowful part, the evil part, the compassionate part, the noticing part, the reverent part, the irreverent part, the conscious part. From birth to death we shine like stars and then explode, and our lives are recapitulations of that original creating. As a child once told the famous teacher Sophia Lyon Fahs, after studying seeds that became marigolds in a paper cup and after the arrival of a newborn sister, which meant the arrival of both unprecedented hatred and unprecedented tenderness, "God is what knows how to grow."

Each of us tells the story differently, setting our words to music all our own. Your song might not be all this inexplicable nature-mysticism but instead some kind of muscular, articulate agnosticism, or ethical humanism, or atheism, or liberal Christianity, or some kind of Western Buddhism, or an ethical, practical religion based on justice making and real action, or paganism mixed with feminism, or who knows what. God knows what it is. You sing your song in your own key, in your own beautiful voice, and the cosmos listens, reverently.

The story I live by is told to me by the only world that I can see and taste, the world I could begin to describe if I were an artist or a physicist or a dancer or a mathematician: the world that lives and dies in cycles and in seasons. It is an utterly unsupernatural story, an evolving, unfinished story; our part in it is the making of meaning, the making of questions and celebrations, and these too evolve and expand without end.

The Wind Is Bearing Me Across the Sky

Of prayer, Howard Thurman noted, "The preparations vary in accordance with the temper of the person and the gravity of need."

A few years ago a friend of the family had great gravity of need. His partner in life was leaving, and his four teenage children, whom he'd held as babies and loved and raised all this time, had all but stopped speaking to him. He's a baker and an artist, and his business was in tatters. "Did you know that *dis-aster* literally means 'falling star?'" he asked us at one point. One night in the midst of the maelstrom of *asters* crashing all around, he called to tell us about an anonymous note someone had mailed to his bakery. We weren't at home, so he read it into our answering machine. "Hey guys. Listen to this note that someone sent today: 'Sir. You have saved my life with bread. Thank you. An old friend.'"

Our friend was silent for a long, long while. (We had a machine that allowed deep silences; it would not disconnect a caller lost momentarily in reverie or caught in contemplation.) Then came his voice again, asking, as if we could answer through the tape, "What do you think of that?" He was quiet, then said, "It makes me think of an old Ojibwe song, the 'Song of the Bird': 'Sometimes I go about in pity for myself, and all the while the wind is bearing me across the sky.'"

That was his whole message, and not long after that, it seemed the stars moved in their courses more reliably, and in time, by grace and his own will, "in accordance with his temper," our friend was healed.

When we are lost or losing ground, it takes discipline and it takes work, spiritual discipline and spiritual work, to get ourselves back home again, to center down, to be quiet and listen for our calling, the voice of God or the voice within that tells us who we are. We must practice with intention, and that's the contemplative work that balances and nourishes any life of activism. But once in a while, by grace or by chance, blessings will come unannounced: a note in the mail, a voice on the tape, a squeeze on your shoulder, a listening ear of a friend who knows and loves you well enough to speak the truth to you and nothing else and nothing less. The way back home when we are lost is a solitary journey—but we are here to encourage one another on that lonely way, and point out signs and markers that weary travelers easily could miss.

Efficiency

One morning, on my way to a monthly professional meeting, I was companioned on the southbound highway by a man in a pickup truck who was brushing his teeth as he drove. He was in the fast lane, I was in the other one, and we both were traveling at about sixty-five miles an hour.

During "sharing time" with my colleagues, I confessed that this metaphor is an apt one for me in the fall: compared with the real (or imagined) lethargy of summer, September is the fast lane. Suddenly there are deadlines again, lots of them, and appointments and events. School starts, everyone leaves for college, and for some reason every major road and artery downtown is being repaved at once. It's a time of year when, if you want your teeth brushed at all, you'd better do it while doing something else of equal import; it's a time of year when the sound of typing fills the background of telephone calls because the person on the other end is writing letters or answering e-mail while we talk.

I understand the impulse and I deeply sympathize (after all, I was finishing a muffin in my lap when my hygienic fellow traveler passed me on the highway), but I know that brushing while you drive is bad religion. Doing almost any two things at once, in the same moment, is bad religion. *Rushing* is bad religion.

And so, as the leaves turn and the apples ripen, I resolve again to *notice*, and bid you notice, too.

I resolve again to go more slowly, to do *one* thing and *then* another, to watch the sky and hear the geese and greet them, as I do every soul I meet, one by one by one by one. . . .

There are hawks to see now on the southbound side, and sumac flaming red; there are skunks, porcupines, the shadows of deer and the tender fog that hugs our mountains, just off the exit heading west.

I will brush my teeth some other time.

At One

Imagine this.

On the days between Rosh Hashanah and Yom Kippur, every fall, every year, the people make their peace with anyone they have wronged or slighted or injured or in any way neglected in the past twelve months. The task is not to patch things up, smooth things over, reach a compromise, or sweep mistakes and uneasy memories under the rug; the task is not to feel better. The task is ownership. The goal is truth, for its own redemptive sake. *I did this. I said this to you, and it was wrong. I neglected this. I botched this. I betrayed you thusly.*

I demeaned you, whether you ever knew it or not.

This is the truth in which both of us are living. I ask you to forgive me.

Imagine how many deep breaths you would need to take. Imagine how many doors you'd have to knock on, how many phone calls you'd have to make, how many letters, how many lunches and coffees, how many awkward moments with your children and your parents, and with strangers (that cashier to whom you spoke so sharply). Awkward is irrelevant. The task is not about comfort, it is about truth, about wholeness and holiness. Restoration.

Imagine this.

Someone has been preparing all year to speak with you, to write to you, to ask you a hard question. Perhaps in some way not quite conscious, you have even known this, and you have been preparing too. Finally, you answer the door or the phone, or open the letter with shaky hands, and there it is, what you thought you'd been longing for but really have dreaded: someone is asking your forgiveness. The task is not about comfort, it is about truth. Awkward is irrelevant. You get to choose now, you have to choose, whether and how you will participate in restoration. Abandon the pleasant piety that claims knee-jerk forgiveness as the unquestioned moral course. You get to choose which way will be right in this case, between you as persons and with all your gods. What response will make the world more whole?

Imagine. Something yearns in us to come round right. Something creaky, rusty, heavy, almost calcified within us tries— in spite of us and of all our fears and self-deceptions—to turn and turn and creak and turn again and come round a little truer. Something in us stretches toward conversion.

Imagine healing, wholly, from within.

Turquoise Patriot

A child I know, when asked whether she would answer the call of her elementary school principal to wear red, white, and blue clothes to school on Thursday, was in a quandary. She put down the crayon with which she was painstakingly trying to squeeze the words *peace is possible* onto the white bars between the red bars on the small American flag she had made, and said, "Well, it *is* a pretty good country . . . so it's hard to know what to wear."

This *is* a pretty good country. It is one of hundreds and hundreds of pretty good countries, layered relatively recently onto the skim of topsoil or desert sand or water that covers our globe. It is one of hundreds of pretty good countries filled with millions of pretty good and proud and worthy people, these other lands with sunlight, too, and clover. It's a pretty good but pretty complicated country, where lately I, who am a lifelong citizen, feel even more than usual like an alien, afraid that if I speak, my voice might betray not some foreign place of origin but the uneven geography of my heart. It *is* hard to know what to wear.

And what to say. These days everywhere I go, with anyone I meet, I'm wondering, where are you coming from, friend, with your black armband, with your flag, with your red, white, and blue clothing, with your peace sign, with your tears? What roads have you traveled to reach the place where you are? In our pretty good country it is an honor and a privilege to answer and in turn to ask, what really are we loyal to? What usefulness can nationalism serve now, as the old world yields to a new century? What is America's right relation and right role, and my right role as a citizen? And what are you going to wear?

The child found her own remarkable response. When asked what she thought she'd like to do, she did say, "It's a pretty good country," and she looked up then for confirmation of that claim, for some assurance that this guess might in fact be true—and this I gladly gave her. (She knows I have my doubts but needs to be reminded, just as I do, that they go hand in hand with hopes and dreams so passionate, so powerful.) And then she said, deeply serious, without seeking my collaboration or permission, "I think I'm gonna wear turquoise, pink, and beige for now." And so she did, and I don't know if she knows what risk might be entailed there, what wrath she may incur among her playground comrades or her teachers or her principal, or how her own chosen symbols of ambivalence might be misunderstood. I don't know what confidence she may inspire, in this country to which she has not yet even learned, at her young age, to pledge allegiance. For now she is a turquoise patriot; she's proud and scared and questioning; her allegiance is to her own conscience; and her trust is, for now, with the adults, in whose clumsy hands her entire future is contained.

Any Other Questions?

People ask me sometimes, "Is this a gay church?"

It is a privilege to answer: "Ours is absolutely, gladly, hopefully and humbly, gaily, a gay church, a gay tradition, where everyone, including heterosexual members and friends, is welcome, where everyone is needed, where everyone's experience is cherished as a sacred text, because no one's experience of living or loving can be comprehensive, because each of us holds clues the others need about how to live with dignity and joy as a human person, and none of us knows enough about that yet to be considered whole.

"It is absolutely a gay church, even as ours is a gay world, if you would look around. Gay church, straight church, peoples' church, a human congregation made holy by the holy hopes and fears and dreams of all who wish to come. Come in, we say. Come out, come in. We're all in this together."

I will not speak of "tolerance," with its courteous clenched teeth and bitter resignation. I will not speak about "acceptance," of "other" people and some "other" kind of "lifestyle." I can only look in laughing wonder at human life in all its incarnations. I can taste only in passing the breath of the spirit of life on my mouth and understand our common longing to breathe in deep, deep gulps of it. I cannot think of being anybody else's "ally," even, because even that implies some degree of separation—some degree of safety for some of us, not all. We are "allied" with no one and with nothing but love—the larger Love transcending all our understanding, within which all the different, differing, gorgeously various, variant, beautifully deviant aspects of ourselves are bound in elegant unity.

I know that on some sad and disappointing days these words describe the church that *yet shall be* and not the church that *is*. I know, I know. . . . But I know too that to answer is an act of creation. To answer this question, and some others, is a privilege, a prophetic imperative, a joy, a duty, and a holy sacrament.

Who Do You Think You Are?

So last Sunday, when we were all singing "Amazing Grace," and we got to that bizarre moment in the first verse where our Unitarian Universalist hymnbook slaps down an asterisk and a choice, what did you do? Which did you choose to sing: "Amazing grace, how sweet the sound that saved a *wretch* like me" or ". . . that saved a *soul* like me"?

It probably depends on how you were feeling that day, how particularly wretched or soulful. I know of no other hymnal in print that virtually stops the singing in mid-measure to poll the congregation, to call for a theological debate within the mind and heart of every singer. And right there, quickly, because the pianist isn't going to wait for you, the congregation isn't going to wait for you, Sunday rolling on its way to Monday isn't going to wait for you, you have to stake your claim, make your mark, testify—all the while wondering if the person singing next to you will take offense if you confess at the top of your voice your own wretchedness and even our common condition as a fallen, faulty species. Or will your neighbor be annoyed, or maybe shocked, if you stand there warbling on about what a pleasant soul you are, what a nice, well-rounded, fully individuated, sin-free, guilt-free humanist soul? There you stand, frozen in time, and the music plays on while you hastily cobble a theology.

We sing our song in different keys and cadences. We are on our own to make a faith out of nothing, which is to say, out of everything we have. That is daunting, lonely work, demanding and relentless work, the work of a lifetime, and I suspect it is the very scope of it that keeps our tiny movement small. Not everyone wants to stop singing in the middle of the song and consider once again and all alone the nature of the human soul and God, infinity without and infinity within.

It's a lot to ask of people on a Sunday morning.

Stung by Bees

A young child is stung by hornets on a playground on a summer morning, joining the ranks of children everywhere. It's her first time and she takes it very personally. Weeks after the fact, out of nowhere, she asks, "*why* was I stung by bees?" "Why was *I* stung by bees?" Her mind requires the why, she is not at peace with her vast unknowing, and she is only momentarily satisfied when for the 107th time I explain, "You were stung by bees because they were on the play structure at exactly the same time as you."

"Were they mean bees?" she says. I say no.

"Are bees bad?" I tell her no.

"Are they supposed to sting us?" I say, "Not exactly."

"Well, then, why was I stung by bees?"

She is a novice philosopher. For the moment, because she is only three years old, there is no way to explain random chance and luck and the doctrine of grace, no way to say, "Look. It just happened. You and the hornets got there together, okay? It was just an accident." She lives in the endless echoing of "why." She relies, like many of us, on the illusion of cause and effect in this life to make sense of it, to get her bearings. There is no real way just yet to interest her as deeply in mystery and in the far more serious, echoing question, which is, "So what will you do now?"

Will you always be scared of bees? Do you still love to look at insects? Would you like to learn more about bees and wasps and hornets, or maybe steer clear for a while, move on to ants and beetles, a safer entomology? Shall we put up a sign to warn other children?

She's trapped, as I so often am, in *why* it happened, and how. But so much more, so much worth wondering and pondering, lies in what will happen next.

Who made the world, the broken world, and why? Who made the suffering world, and why? Three-year-olds and theologians can chew these tired bones all day. But for me the real religious questions open wide and holy—exciting, dangerous, urgent, comforting, sustaining—when we accept the mystery and then move on or, reverently, move in.

The world was made—gorgeous, tender, broken, dangerous—we know not why.

How now shall we live in it, you and I and everyone?

The Gold Stars and the Bittersweet

One afternoon someone left a strange and beautiful message scotch-taped to the office door. The author didn't even leave a name, though I knew who it was; her message simply said, "I forgot to tell you when we met this morning, there are little gold stars all amongst the bittersweet. It's all there, mixed together." I had just met with this person, who was not quite in crisis but dancing on the edge, talking and weeping and raging through one of those hard, hard moments that can last for weeks or months or years. It was painful stuff, faced with courage. Here, hours later, was this slightly mysterious, elegant message, and I thought how amazing it is that some people can render even the most desperate experience poetically, and what a gift this is, this making of art out of ashes, and how rare. I was very moved.

The next day, there came a second message from the same person on the answering machine, slightly altering my view of things. "It's me again, calling back about the stars and bittersweet. I forgot to tell you, I stuffed it all in garbage bags, and they're in the closet in the Social Hall. Those berries make an awful mess."

Well, there's not much poetry in that. As it turns out, there were no metaphors at work at all. Before our appointment that morning, this person had been cleaning up after a church party, for which the decorations had included branches of cut bittersweet from members' autumn gardens and long lengths of gold tinsel wire to which tiny metal stars were fixed. So it really was all garbage.

But I'm intrigued by conversations and by language that can speak of trash bags, closets, golden stars and bittersweet, and refer with equal accuracy to the very depths of human hope and suffering or to the details of committee cleanup. And I know that I am called—as I suspect we all are called—to places where the sacred and the ordinary are all mixed up together, where work is prayer and prayer is song and songs are sacraments and sacraments are silent or spoken brokenly in messages we sometimes barely comprehend, in words we speak in love to one another and to the golden stars.

Table Blessing

At my house at supper we perform the most unholy and untidy little liturgy you can imagine, but usually I think it works. Other families, I know, conduct their affairs with more elegance and style, but elegance is not our strength.

At our house, the table grace we do does not look like religion; it looks like a hungry, tattered family at the end of a tattered day, sometimes at the end of its rope. We scramble to find the matches, to clear and set the table, to dislodge the cats and scrape our chairs into place. We clatter in, then get up again to wash somebody's hands, then finally sit down. We light the candles, reach for each other's hands, close our eyes, and sit in silence for as long as the youngest among us can stand it, which is generally up to as high as she can count. Then, on most nights, we sing something: "Dona Nobis Pacem," "Jubilate Deo," "Shalom," the Mozart Alleluia, "Old Hundredth," "Over the River and Through the Woods," "The Wheels on the Bus Go Round and Round," "Taps." We try to be serious, but really, it does not matter what we sing.

We are in a self-imposed time-out. The smell of the food becomes real. The sound of our breath and the feel of our damp hands, still sticky, these are real. We are together, our circle invincible in this one holy moment, and each of us utterly alone in the dark solitude behind closed eyes. We are home, we have food. We recall that many don't, and sometimes someone says this in a blessing. And where we have been in the day and where we may go that night or tomorrow fades away for a time, and we are infused, and time is infused, and something wells up. Something like gratitude wells up, overflowing, nigh unto overwhelming. The whole thing lasts, from candle to song, about two minutes, but the echo, the wake of it, lasts longer.

We are trying (all of us, in all our houses) to be aware.

We are trying to be quiet.

We are trying to slow down.

We are trying to remember our true and real life. We are trying to touch that, to call it up, trying to know we are alive, hoping to mold that knowing into good work—hopeful, brave, and helpful later on. We are trying to remember what we love and what to do, and how to be ourselves, good gifts.

Subversive Suburban Soul

My family's favorite place to view the sunset is a place where the westbound highway meets the main commercial artery of our suburban city. There is a vast expanse of parking lot between the mammoth supermarket and the monstrous home improvement store. It is one deeply unholy place, with miles of sprawling strip malls as far as the eye can see, and farther: a perfect paradise of asphalt, greed, and thoughtless multinational development. Yet more than once, on leaving the store, I have all but fallen to my knees there because the sunsets are astonishing, and on evenings when the full moon rises, they are breathtaking. There's just enough elevation, and the buildings, awful as they are, are perfectly positioned, however accidentally. (I wonder, will archeologists of the future unearth this site someday and think that it's just like Stonehenge, with these mysterious monoliths—big, boxy megastores—laid out in such a magic way that sun and moon are honored, and sacred light comes streaming down?)

This unlikely and unholy hill offers so startling and memorable a view that one time in the summer, when my family was camping in a far-removed, wild wilderness, watching the sun melt down to the sea, my daughter sighed blissfully, snuggled closer, and said, "Wow. This is so beautiful. This really reminds me of the shopping center on Highway 36." It was then that we knew we were living a little too close to so-called civilization.

What makes a place a holy place? How much is what is there, and how much is what we bring, or what we choose to see? Now I've been told that this parking lot is set upon a hill that not so long ago—perhaps 150 years ago—was in fact a sacred site for the native peoples living on this land, a stopping place between one great river and another. A few remember that there was an ancient stand of oaks up here. It is known that the sun went down, and heaven and the prairie were engulfed each night in flames. It is known that the moon came up in splendor.

Beneath the pavement, earth remembers. Everything—every thing—is gathered in, for it is known, it is remembered, that the holy holds all weeping as well as all celebration, all desecration as well as all tenderness. Every thing is gathered in. How could a place once sacred at once be rendered otherwise?

I know that if I leave an offering among the SUVs and shopping carts, a branch or shell or little stone to mark the ache inside me, to signal reverence, sorrow, and confusion, I may be charged with littering. I know, and do it anyway.

Trees for Starters

A child in our Sunday School was overheard to say about his church, "I don't know the name of it, but where we go we're really interested in trees. All of us believe in trees." His mother called us shortly afterward to report this unusual confession of the faith, and to see whether we thought it was time to supplement her boy's understanding with a more comprehensive Unitarian Universalist theology.

I don't know if there is a more comprehensive Unitarian Universalist theology. All of us believe in trees. Like my young comrade, that little Buddha back in New York state, I've always been "very interested in trees," meaning I have always (as far back as I can remember) had a spiritual orientation that unfolds itself, reveals itself outside, and inside, and it cannot be contained within any single creed or book or building or tradition, and it cannot respond, and never has, to small-minded anthropomorphic gods in beards or turbans or suits and ties, these deities who are larger than life but smaller than soul. They have never spoken to me in words that I can understand. Even as a tiny girl, singing, "Jesus loves me, this I know, for the Bible tells me so," I remember thinking maybe there is a Jesus and maybe there is an embracing love, immortal, invisible, radiating through the cosmos, touching even me—but if there is, it cannot be because the Bible tells me so; it must be deeper, older, wider, wilder, more reliable than that. I remember wanting those sky gods to rise up from their thrones and become little birds, flying up beyond the sky to fix themselves as stars, or fluttering down to earth, spilling down as drops of rain splashing on my hand." Even as a child I knew, and perhaps most clearly then: A throne is no place for a god.

Which is not to say that I was deaf, for I was not, to all the stories, songs, and psalms, the mysteries and ethical teachings out of all of those traditions of the West and of the East, which do speak to my heart and open it continuously (including, absolutely, Jesus, and the radical love, *agape,* at the core of Christian mysticism—absolutely, and why not?). But for me these are just windows through which we can gaze upon and sometimes apprehend the sacred; they are not the thing itself.

Even stars and water, even trees, are not quite the thing itself.

Open Eyes

To see, simply to look and to see, is an ethical act and intentional choice; to see, with open eyes, is a spiritual practice and thus a risk, for it can open you to ways of knowing the world and loving it that will lead to inevitable consequences. The awakened eye is a conscious eye, a willful eye, and brave, because to see things as they are, each in its own truth, will make you very vulnerable.

Think of yourself as a prism made of glass, reflecting everything exactly as it is, unable to exist dishonestly—reflecting beauty where there's beauty, violence where there's violence, loveliness and unexpected joy where there is joy, violation where there's violation.

Here's the front page of the paper; here's that seedy, gossipy conflict at your job; here's a memory, unblurred by wishful thinking; here's a perfect afternoon in spring, and buds now on the trees, and blackbirds in the marsh. Here's the world, just as it is—now look!

That kind of seeing is a choice, and it is a sacred practice.

And then there is refraction—taking into yourself, as a prism takes in light, the truth of what you see and hear and transforming it somehow, changing its direction, acting on it, rendering it somehow, anew. That again is holy work. The spring day, received, comes out again as gratitude (dispersed into a spectrum); a sorrow, yours or someone else's, fully realized and received, not denied, not covered up, not justified or explained away, ignored—some sorrow clearly, bravely seen is taken in, absorbed and felt, and reemerges, bent now into compassion. To see clearly is an act of will and conscience. It will make you very vulnerable. It is persistent, holy, world-transforming work.

In Between

One afternoon some time ago I brought my little baby out to visit a very, very old neighbor who was dying that year, quietly and gracefully, in her gracious home. We were having a little birthday party for her, with sherry and cake and a few old friends gathered round her bed. To free a hand to cut the cake, I put my baby down right on the bed, right up on the pillow—and there was a sudden hush in the room, for we were caught off guard, beholding.

It was a startling sight. There in the late afternoon light were two people side by side, two human merely beings. Neither one could walk, neither one could speak, not in language you could understand, both utterly dependent on the rest of us bustling around, masquerading as immortals. There they were: a plump one, apple-cheeked, a cherry tomato of a babe, smiling; and a silver-thin one, hollow-eyed, translucent, shining, smiling. We revelers were hushed because we clearly saw that these were dancers on the very edge of things. These two were closer to the threshold, the edge of the great mystery, than any of us had been for a long time or would be for a while. Living, breathing, smiling they were, but each with one foot and who knows how much consciousness firmly planted on the other side, whatever that is, wherever that is, the starry darkness from whence we come and whither we will go, in time. Fresh from birth, nigh unto death, bright-eyed, they were bookends there, mirrors of each other. Radiant.

Cake in hand, and napkins, knife, glasses, a crystal carafe a century old, we paused there on the thresholds of our own momentary lives. Then, "What shall we sing?" said someone, to the silence, to the sunlight on the covers, to the stars. It was the only question, then, as now, years later. What on earth shall we sing?

Immortal, Invisible

Where do they go, do you think, when they die? Our mothers and brothers and lovers, grandfathers, colleagues, children, and friends? You turn your head and suddenly they have slipped away—but where? What's happened? How could we. . . ? How could they. . . ?

What remains?

I find myself telling a young child things I didn't know I believe about death, things that shock me, make me wonder. We come across a small dead turtle in the road and we decide to bury it. So with a stick we scrape a space on the edge of someone else's grass and put the little disk of shell in the hollow of the earth, and I tell what will happen to the turtle, to the muscle and the blood and the eyes and the shell. He loves this. "It all goes back to the earth," I say, "into new soil, and new plants will use it and grow, and birds will eat the plants, or we will, and the birds will scatter seeds, which turtles might eat, round and round and round it goes." This much I know is true. But I also say, because clearly the child is waiting to hear more, clearly he knows that this cannot not be all: "And the spirit of the turtle comes out and goes back into everything, into the stars and the sun and you and me. Everything the turtle was returns to everything and it is not lost."

We're both a little shocked at that, and pondering, as we continue walking.

That same child was told not long ago by a well-meaning relative that her dead cat (the relative's dead cat) is happy now in "kitty heaven." And the fact is, though I roll my supercilious eyes and make derisive noises, I don't know now and never will whether "kitty heaven" is real (or "kitty hell," for that matter). The child and I, and all the poets and philosophers, the scientists and scholars, are equal in our ignorance on this and equal in our expertise when someone asks, "What will happen to the turtle?"—or to us. Bowel and blood and bone change into other things—dust and drop and molecule—but what about the soul? The heart is water and flesh; it decomposes fast, or burns. But what of the heart's contents?

What we know for sure when someone dies is loneliness. What we know is the lifelong struggle to remember. What we know, beyond biology and chemistry, what we know forever and ever are the questions: what remains of him, of her, what remains of you . . . in me?

Set in Stone

In a cemetery once, an old one in New England, I found a strangely soothing epitaph. The name of the deceased and her dates had been scoured away by wind and rain, but there was a carving of a tree with roots and branches (a classic nineteenth-century motif) and among them the words, "She attended well and faithfully to a few worthy things." At first this seemed to me a little meager, a little stingy on the part of her survivors, but I wrote it down and have thought about it since, and now I can't imagine a more proud or satisfying legacy.

"She attended well and faithfully to a few worthy things."

Every day I stand in danger of being struck by lightning and having the obituary in the local paper say, for all the world to see, "She attended frantically and ineffectually to a great many unimportant, meaningless details."

How do you want your obituary to read?

"He got all the dishes washed and dried before playing with his children in the evening."

"She balanced her checkbook with meticulous precision and never missed a day of work—missed a lot of sunsets, missed a lot of love, missed a lot of risk, missed a lot—but her money was in order."

"She answered all her calls, all her e-mail, all her voice-mail, but along the way she forgot to answer the call to service and compassion, and forgiveness, first and foremost of herself."

"He gave and forgave sparingly, without radical intention, without passion or conviction."

"She could not, or would not, hear the calling of her heart."

How will it read, how does it read, and if you had to name a few worthy things to which you attend well and faithfully, what, I wonder, would they be?

The Moment of Magic

Now is the moment of magic,
when the whole, round earth turns again toward the sun,

    and here's a blessing:
the days will be longer and brighter now,
even before the winter settles in to chill us.

Now is the moment of magic,
when people beaten down and broken,
with nothing left but misery and candles and their own clear voices,
kindle tiny lights and whisper secret music,

    and here's a blessing:
the dark universe is suddenly illuminated by the lights of the menorah,
suddenly ablaze with the lights of the kinara,
and the whole world is glad and loud with winter singing.

Now is the moment of magic,
when an eastern star beckons the ignorant toward an unknown goal,

    and here's a blessing:
they find nothing in the end but an ordinary baby,
born at midnight, born in poverty, and the baby's cry, like bells ringing,
makes people wonder as they wander through their lives,

what human love might really look like,
sound like,
feel like.

Now is the moment of magic,

    and here's a blessing:
we already possess all the gifts we need;
we've already received our presents:
ears to hear music,
eyes to behold lights,
hands to build true peace on earth
and to hold each other tight in love.

In the Struggle, Singing, Shining

I once saw a little girl dressed in a fabulous outfit. She was in preschool, and her clothes were matched only by the radiance with which she wore them—a dress tie-dyed in bright orange, hot pink, and electric yellow, with socks to match, pink suede sandals, and on her knee, as she revealed to me demurely by lifting the hem of her skirt, a Band-Aid in the brightest bright blue. "We were out of purple ones," she explained with mild regret. The child was shining, shining. I admired her dress and her joie de vivre, and she said, "Well, I wanted to wear my favorite outfit because we were having church today, and [in case I somehow failed to guess it] this *is* my favorite outfit." She gave her dress a little flip and smoothed her bunchy bodice. She straightened her short legs so the sandals stuck straight out. She ratcheted up those fiery socks and looked me in the eye. I thanked her humbly for her example, and wholeheartedly I meant it.

Later, in the afterglow of her costume and her gladness, I thought about that girl. There are children all over this world, and some adults, scattered here and there, who unfailingly will punctuate their lives and their days with sacred celebration and with rituals signifying joy, no matter what they have—or don't—to work with, no matter what fury the world outside is howling. They will savor life and breath and all their days no matter what is dealt them. It's the only way some people know to live—with gladness and cacophonous color. These are people who pray without ceasing, awake and aware, chanting (if they're old enough), "This is the life I'd risk anything to save."

"Gather yourselves," say the Hopi elders. "See who is in the water with you and celebrate. All that we do now must be done in a sacred manner and in celebration."

There are things in this life that are so beautiful, so lovely, so simple—extraordinarily ordinary blessings—that the only response sometimes is thankfulness, the kind of thankfulness that clamors for loud colors on a Sunday.

Choose your clothing with defiance, with attitude, with joie de vivre and with intention. Every action is a sacrament, every move a symbol, every color is a song. This is a day we'd risk anything to save.

Why Do You Come, John?

I knew a man once who came to church every Sunday. You may find nothing remarkable in this. But think of it—a man who came every single Sunday, and it was not that he lacked other things to do. I knew him only in the last years of his life—a birthright Unitarian, a retired geologist who, when he was not at church, was a volunteer for Amnesty International, for the local food bank, for the American Civil Liberties Union, for the family planning clinic, the AIDS project, for the Unitarian Universalist district we were part of, for the Audubon Society, and for a splendid community chorus. Busier than any of us still holding full-time jobs, he was committed, effective, clear about what he could and would and, by his own standards, should contribute to the causes that he cared for, the world and people that he cared for. But what set him apart from all of us was that he came every single Sunday, and (because of hearing loss, I think, more than any sense of his own importance) he sat in the front row.

"Why do you come, John? In all kinds of weather, when you're well and when you're not, when you like the guest speaker and when you know you won't, why do you come every Sunday?" I asked him not long before he died. His answer was straightforward, just like the man himself. "I come," he said, "because somebody might miss me if I didn't."

He said it in a way not arrogant at all, but generously, and honestly. He was the kind of person who saw it as his duty and his privilege to welcome newcomers on Sunday morning—not because he needed more friends himself (the man was eighty years old, with a lifetime of friends and colleagues and acquaintances to spare; he had plenty of friends already, more than he could handle). He did it not because he wanted to evangelize the visitors or grow the church (on the contrary, he loved and missed the tiny congregation he'd joined in 1955. He felt a little lost with so many new faces, a little sad at all the changes). He greeted people as they came, and steered them toward the minister, the coffee pot, the Sunday School, the guest book, the pledge cards, the sign-up sheets, because he felt it was the right and only thing to do. When people come into your home, you welcome them as if nothing in that moment matters more. He worked hard on Sunday mornings, he got up on Sundays expecting to work hard to make others feel at home; he came with that in mind. And he was right—after he died, we missed him when he didn't come.

And do you know what happened? The Sunday after his memorial, someone new (who'd never met John Eric and now would never have the chance) walked right in and sat down in his empty place in that front row. A whole family just sat right down as if they owned the place, as if they had every right to be there, as if we were glad to see them—two women new to town, and their toddler and their baby. They came hoping there was room, and John himself would have been delighted.

Women Walking in Loud Shoes

On a Saturday I went to a hospital in the city to make a visit to a patient. This was a big place, and as always I managed to park as far as I could from where I needed to be, and so took myself on an accidental tour of the entire hospital campus, through miles of corridors and hallways, most of which were deserted because it was the weekend. I was wearing new shoes, sort of fancy shoes, and suddenly became aware of what a racket I was making in those empty hallways, clickety-clacketing in loud, lonely, staccato echoes, sounding either very important or very clumsy or both, and either way, ridiculous.

I had read an article about the many offenses for which the oppressive Taliban rulers in Afghanistan might arrest and imprison people. Among the crimes was listed "women walking in loud shoes." They could go to jail for that. They could be seized on the street, or in their homes, for that. For some reason this scrap of information floated back to me that Saturday on my long pilgrimage from the parking garage to the critical care unit, and though I did try to go respectfully on tiptoe when I got to floors where patients might be sleeping, I have to confess that in the empty hallways, in the stairwells, the corridors, once or twice, I wanted to see exactly how loud those fancy new shoes could be. And this was not just for fun—I stamped with defiance on the tiles, and that was a noisy prayer and a blessing for the Afghan women.

My walk through all those halls was long enough that I had time to think not only of women's torment by the Taliban but of the thousands killed now by our retaliatory bombing there—women, like us, their children, their old ones, and men. And I had time to think of women in the West Bank, Palestinian women with no shoes at all, terrified Israeli women, Pakistani women, and the women of India, who might or might not be annihilated at any moment by their leaders' arrogance or ignorance. I clattered for them also. I clattered for the women and the babies of Iraq, for the women and the babies everywhere. It was a fearsome sound.

These days it sometimes feels as if stomping our feet is all we can do—but you know, even that can be a sacrament, a first step, as it were; any crazy act of solidarity with sisters halfway round the world (or halfway round the room) can be a prayer, if you're mindful, if you're artful, if you're doing it on purpose. Once you realize that walking in loud shoes (or in any shoes at all, or simply walking, safely, as we do every single day) is a privilege and luxury, then the burden is upon you. The burden of response, of giving back and taking risks for what is right, the burden of courage and clear speaking and clear thinking, the burden of gratitude and compassion, is on you, and one thing leads to something else.

Memory

I taught once at a farm school in Vermont, where it was the custom on Memorial Day to visit all the little cemeteries in the countryside nearby. There were many of these—some in churchyards or next to open fields where churches used to be, some on windy hillsides, some hidden far back in the woods, overgrown with brush and brambles, dimly defined in the shadows by the remnants of a low stone wall. These expeditions were led by the teacher at the school, a native of the town who remembered where all these forgotten places were. Children and teachers together piled into several cars and went to maybe six or seven graveyards in a day. At the entrance to each one, the teacher had us join hands in two rows of ten or twelve and then slowly walk the grounds, looking out for graves of veterans, many marked by little metal signposts but some so old we had to bend and squint and read the wind-smooth stones. They dated to the Revolutionary War and the War of 1812, the Civil War, the two world wars, and the Korean War; there were a few more recent monuments to men who died in Vietnam. All of these were interspersed, at peace again, with all the town's civilians.

It was a very solemn kind of game. On finding the grave of a veteran, someone would call out, "Here's one, here's one!" and we'd clear the leaves and branches off, replace last year's little faded American flag with a fresh one, and then read out the name and dates. In some of these graveyards there was a little area set off to the side, with smaller stones with no inscriptions—this would be the "colored section," where in the last century African and Native Americans were buried, or Jews sometimes, or unmarried women who died in childbirth, anyone cast out or unwanted. The teacher always put a flag or two in here, and we cleared all the graves because, he said, "Chances are, someone in here was a soldier; and all of them were people." Before leaving every cemetery, we'd gather in a circle and some child would play "Taps" on the recorder, and someone would read a verse from "Flanders Fields," and then we'd stand in silence (the loud silence of birdsong and spring wind), till the teacher would say so quietly that you could barely hear him (he was very shy), "Let us not forget," and we'd move on down the road.

The youngest children with us on those days were remembering things they had not yet even learned, names of people dead in wars they'd never heard of, vast sadnesses their minds could not yet imagine. But even they could grasp it: we were honoring these fallen dead so that someday there would be no more. Together, two dozen souls of mixed age and experience were remembering the future. It was a prayer, though none was spoken.

Incarnation
For Auriel

―∽―

"But it is plain hell," says a woman a thousand years old, whom I know and love, a woman old enough to speak with some authority on matters of the body. She isn't sick so much as frail, a fragile paper casing of her former formidable self, brittle, broken here and there, and fading, physically, away. But the spirit! I know she believes she doesn't have one, but something blazes out of her, something fierce and wild rages out of those eyes now large as lakes in her small face, something that can warm you, or scorch you if you get too close, something shining and more so all the time, with every day she ages. Even in the way she speaks of getting old, so bitingly, bitterly, she becomes more of herself. She is a chrysalis, and as the shell disintegrates the animal itself emerges, all power and dangerous fire. In her case, though, it is the *anima,* of course, I see emerging. I can see this woman's soul. On days when she is feeling strong, we argue about this.

Where does the body end and the woman herself begin? I think surgeons must wonder this a lot. I hope they wonder it a lot. It's hard to tell because body and soul are of a seamless substance, and my friend is what she is—funny, clear, angry, determined, tired, brilliant, alive—because her eighty-seven-year-old body is all these things. This is a person whose infirmities will not be cured. She is as able and as youthful now as she is ever going to be. There is no romanticizing pain. Yet part of her is healed and whole, it seems. Not placid, never resigned—she is mad as hell, and sometimes sad. Yet she moves with a certain authenticity in her antique skeleton, she breathes her shallow and defiant breaths with respect for inevitable circumstances, neither acquiescent nor violently resisting.

The Quakers at one time had a custom of greeting one another not with our rhetorical "How are you?" but with a different, more demanding question: "How is it with thy spirit?"

This is what I want to ask her now, if I can find some words that she can hear.

How is it with thy spirit and with thy body, soul, and mind? I ask because I cannot tell, I can't possibly tell, by merely looking at you, friend, and I really want to know. From deep in here, in this bonehouse where I dwell alone, I wish to touch and know you, deep in there, still beautiful.

If I Were Asked

If I were asked to confess my faith or my beliefs out loud, and I were scrambling for some place to begin, I would start in the desert, in the lonesome valley, and say that first of all and ultimately we are alone. No god abides with us, caring, watching, mindful of our going out and coming in. The only certainty is mystery. We are alone, and because we are alone it is the chance connections, both chosen and involuntary, that matter most of all and ultimately help and heal and hold us.

We are alone yet intricately bound, inextricably connected to soil and stream and forest, to sun and corn and melting snow. We are alone yet bound by stories we cannot get out of to ancestors and descendants we will never meet. And all these natural conditions, these bonds we did not forge ourselves and yet cannot deny, are the strands of a theology, the seeds of faith, the beginning of *re-ligion*, of binding all things.

When I say *God*—and sometimes I do, because sometimes there is no other metaphor, no other symbol, no other poetry, no other offering—when I say *God* I mean that place of meeting, that place where solitudes join. The space between my hand and that dogwood, the space where the tiny feet of the ant brush the dry dirt beneath her, the space between Mercury and Venus, between electrons, which we unblinkingly believe in without seeing. *God* is the space in between, the bridge between solitudes, the ground where we meet, you and I, or any two, by grace.

If I were asked I'd say that all of us, together, are alone, and the emptiness between us is waiting to be filled.

Desert Spring

They had no idea where they were going, when they left that night, in the dark, without lights, without shoes, without bread, their children smothered against them so they would make no noise.

They had no idea what they were getting into, following this Moses, this wild-eyed one who claimed visions and made promises but who after all could guarantee them nothing, except death if they were caught.

They had no idea, these slaves, what it could mean, this promise of land (their own country) and life abundant. Of freedom they knew nothing, except what they could taste by living in its opposite, slavery, and that taste became a hunger, and that hunger became insatiable till they were ravenous for freedom, and they went out then—but no one knows to this day whether they were led by Moses or by the outstretched arm and mighty hand of something else, of something eternal (as they would afterwards and always claim), or whether their own human, hungry will made them flee that night from Pharaoh.

They went into the wilderness. There they wandered forty years, which in those days was a lifetime. Forty was a good, old age, so many of them died before getting anywhere, and many were born in the desert and grew to adulthood knowing nothing but the journey—not slavery, not freedom, just the going. They whined and complained and muttered, and some mutinied, for they were a stiff-necked and rebellious people (you can read it for yourself); ungrateful people, even when manna rained down from heaven and quails were sent to feed them; unhappy people, longing, out loud even, for the familiar security of Egypt, of all places, where at least they knew what to expect, as awful as it was; impatient people, making cheap little idols and gods of metal to bargain with in secret when the traveling got hard or merely dull, and the days and years became monotonous.

In the springtime we remember: the promised land is not a destination—it is a way of going. The land beyond the Jordan, that country of freedom and dignity and laughter—you carry it inside you all the while. It is planted in your mind and heart already, before you ever start out, before it even occurs to you that in order to leave that life in Egypt, the intolerable bondage of that life, what you need to do is stand up and walk forward.

Did the Sun Come Up This Morning?

The dead shall rise again.

Have you seen the trees? Have you seen the maple buds? The magnolias, swelling? Poplars, the first lacy, pale spray across the shoulder of the hills? The forsythia (or as one child I know calls it, the three-sythia, the two-sythia), and those three small, flowering, perfect crabapple trees in the park, strong little trees begging children to climb them and get lost for a while in their magical, pink canopies?

Did you smell the rain this week, and the muddy, ready earth receiving it? Did you smell the musty, lusty, moldy pile of leaves all thawed now, and underneath, the moist and living earthworms, wide awake?

Is it safe, I wonder, to presume that we have all seen the dead resurrected? Can we presume, just quietly among us, this basic fact? Can we admit, however carefully at first, however foolish it may sound, that once or twice in our lives or perhaps over and over and tumbling over, we have seen events miraculous? Choose the words you will, whatever words you need. If "miracle" cloys, try "unexpected." "Surprising." "Unanticipated." "Lucky." "That which has been given us, that second chance, that second wind, by the grace of God knows what."

The dead shall rise again.

We know, because we've seen it.

We don't know, and never will, where the leaf's strength comes from in the spring. We don't know, and never will, entirely, where our own strength comes from. But we have known despair, some of us, and deep discouragement, some of us, and discord of the mind and heart, or disasters in the body or the spirit or in both. We have known dead hope, dead courage, dead caring, dead will, dead faith, dead vision, dead power, deep winter, and we have felt, perhaps when we least expected to feel anything at all, our own slow blood stir in the vein like maple sap, and something very small and tight within begin to swell and open up, urgent, imperceptible at first, then undeniable—*love lives again that with the dead has been.*

Did the sun come up this morning, no thanks to us and all for us, and did the earth awake again, or did it not?

We will testify to resurrection.

Necessities

"Well, he broke my nose last time, so I'm thinking I should leave."

That is what a woman said to me not long ago in my office when I asked her if she felt any physical threat from the man she was running from. She'd come in looking for the number of a shelter, something she had never done before.

She was carrying her jacket, nothing else. That morning she fled her home and her husband with just a jacket, and she was laughing through tears at how absurd that was. But it was clear that she'd brought other things also, that there were things she'd smuggled out to carry on the journey:

Fear. Just about tangible—fear of what she was leaving and fear of where in the world she might be going. Where would she be sleeping? Fear like a burden on her back but also like a driving engine.

Courage. Connected to the fear.

Emptiness and loneliness, the roaring of adrenaline, nervous energy. Everything about this morning was so new to her.

And she carried something else. She said, "You know, I am so anxious in my home that I can't even say my prayers in the morning." (She comes from another country and from a tradition where such prayers and praises matter.) So she took a jacket and her courage and her fear, her dignity and clarity, and her morning prayers, still beautifully intact, like precious china but more durable; like jewels but more ordinary, more useful; like tools for basic survival but more lovely, more private, more delicate. These things were a lot, I thought, for one woman to carry by herself, but I'm thinking that they may also be just enough.

I don't expect to see her again, except in memory, except in prayer, except in my own solitary searching for sources of conviction.

Map of the Journey in Progress

Here is where I found my voice and chose to be brave.

Here's a place where I forgave someone, against my better judgment, and I survived that, and unexpectedly, amazingly, I became wiser.

Here's where I was once forgiven, was ready for once in my life to receive forgiveness and to be transformed. And I survived that also. I lived to tell the tale.

This is the place where I said *no*, more loudly than I'd thought I ever could, and everybody stared, but I said *no* loudly anyway, because I knew it must be said, and those staring settled down into harmless, ineffective grumbling, and over me they had no power anymore.

Here's a time, and here's another, when I laid down my fear and walked right on into it, right up to my neck into that roiling water.

Here's where cruelty taught me something. And here's where I was first astonished by gratuitous compassion and knew it for the miracle it was, the requirement it is. It was a trembling time.

And here, much later, is where I returned the blessing, clumsily. It wasn't hard, but I was unaccustomed. It cycled round, and as best I could I sent it back on out, passed the gift along.

This circular motion, around and around, has no apparent end.

Here's a place, a murky puddle, where I have stumbled more than once and fallen. I don't know yet what to learn there.

On this site I was outraged and the rage sustains me still; it clarifies my seeing.

And here's where something caught me—a warm breeze in late winter, birdsong in late summer.

Here's where I was told that something was wrong with my eyes, that I see the world strangely, and here's where I said, "Yes, I know, I walk in beauty."

Here is where I began to look with my own eyes and listen with my ears and sing my own song, shaky as it is.

Here is where, if by surgeon's knife, my heart was opened up—and here, and here, and here, and here. These are the landmarks of conversion.

Credo For Now

I believe that whatever else the human purpose may be, that part of it is to notice and to love this universe, to notice and respond with heart and mind and soul and all our sense to the beauty and order of all these living and inanimate things.

I believe that those same traits that enable us to love and to notice, those great gifts that distinguish us from other animals, namely reason, will, and passion, might also lead to our destruction.

I believe, therefore, that compassion, reverence, and humility are necessary disciplines, survival strategies we have to learn.

I believe that no creator fashioned this cosmos and that we cannot know most things. Mystery and ignorance are the rule of life.

I believe that the only model or clue available to us is the model of creation itself. What we know, empirically, is the gorgeous creativity of the unfolding universe and especially the earth. When we have doubts about our calling, it might be wise simply to imitate the creative impulse of the cosmos, to join with it, to act like stars, which live and shine for no other purpose than to explode and die, contributing their energy to some larger, timeless process.

I believe that risk unto death matters. That the creative impulse matters and thus that art and childbearing and teaching and ethics all matter.

I believe that the suffering and death of living things is part of a grand and natural cycle, tragic only because we alone among the animals are so aware of mortality and time. Death is not a part of happiness at all, but it makes clear the urgency of joy.

This is all, for now, today, this afternoon, so far.

Unitarian Universalist Meditation Manuals

Unitarians and Universalists have been publishing annual editions of prayer collections and meditation manuals for 150 years. In 1841 the Unitarians broke with their tradition of addressing only theological topics and published *Short Prayers for the Morning and Evening of Every Day in the Week, with Occasional Prayers and Thanksgivings*. Over the years, the Unitarians published many volumes of prayers, including Theodore Parker's selections. In 1938 *Gaining a Radiant Faith* by Henry H. Saunderson launched the current tradition of an annual Lenten manual.

Several Universalist collections appeared in the early nineteenth century. A comprehensive *Book of Prayers* was published in 1839, featuring both public and private devotions. During the late 1860s, the Universalist Publishing House was founded to publish denominational materials. Like the Unitarians, the Universalists published Lenten manuals, and in the 1950s they complemented this series with Advent manuals.

Since 1961, the year the Unitarians and the Universalists consolidated, the Lenten manual has evolved into a meditation manual, reflecting the theological diversity of the two denominations. Today the Unitarian Universalist Association meditation manuals include two styles of collections: poems or short prose pieces written by one author—usually a Unitarian Universalist minister—and anthologies of works by many authors.

2002	*Instructions in Joy* Nancy Shaffer
	Roller-skating as a Spiritual Discipline Christopher Buice
2001	*This Piece of Eden* Vanessa Rush Southern
	Dancing in the Empty Spaces David O. Rankin
2000	*Glad to Be Human* Kaaren Anderson
	Out of the Ordinary Gordon B. McKeeman
1999	*The Rock of Ages at the Taj Mahal* Meg Barnhouse
	Morning Watch Barbara Pescan
1998	*Glory, Hallelujah! Now Please Pick Up Your Socks* Jane Ellen Mauldin
	Evening Tide Elizabeth Tarbox
1997	*A Temporary State of Grace* David S. Blanchard
	Green Mountain Spring and Other Leaps of Faith Gary A. Kowalski
1996	*Taking Pictures of God* Bruce T. Marshall
	Blessing the Bread Lynn Ungar
1995	*In the Holy Quiet of This Hour* Richard S. Gilbert
1994	*In the Simple Morning Light* Barbara Rohde
1993	*Life Tides* Elizabeth Tarbox
	The Gospel of Universalism Tom Owen-Towle
1992	*Noisy Stones* Robert R. Walsh
1991	*Been in the Storm So Long* Mark Morrison-Reed and Jacqui James, Editors
1990	*Into the Wilderness* Sara Moores Campbell
1989	*A Small Heaven* Jane Ranney Rzepka
1988	*The Numbering of Our Days* Anthony Friess Perrino
1987	*Exaltation* David B. Parke, Editor

1986	*Quest*	Kathy Fuson Hurt
1985	*The Gift of the Ordinary*	Charles S. Stephen, Jr., Editor
1984	*To Meet the Asking Years*	Gordon B. McKeeman, Editor
1983	*Tree and Jubilee*	Greta W. Crosby
1981	*Outstretched Wings of the Spirit*	Donald S. Harrington
1980	*Longing of the Heart*	Paul N. Carnes
1979	*Portraits from the Cross*	David Rankin
1978	*Songs of Simple Thanksgiving*	Kenneth L. Patton
1977	*Promise of Spring*	Clinton Lee Scott
1976	*The Strangeness of This Business*	Clarke D. Wells
1975	*In Unbroken Line*	Chris Raible, Editor
1974	*Stopping Places*	Mary Lou Thompson
1973	*The Tides of Spring*	Charles W. Grady
1972	*73 Voices*	Chris Raible and Ed Darling, Editors
1971	*Bhakti, Santi, Love, Peace*	Jacob Trapp
1970	*Beginning Now*	J. Donald Johnston
1969	*Answers in the Wind*	Charles W. McGehee
1968	*The Trying Out*	Richard Kellaway
1967	*Moments of a Springtime*	Rudolf W. Nemser
1966	*Across the Abyss*	Walter D. Kring
1965	*The Sound of Silence*	Raymond Baughan
1964	*Impassioned Clay*	Ralph Helverson
1963	*Seasons of the Soul*	Robert T. Weston
1962	*The Uncarven Image*	Phillip Hewett
1961	*Parts and Proportions*	Arthur Graham